D0243374
LIBRARIES NI
THDRAWN FROM STOCK

For Augustin

S.B.

First published in 2017 by Nosy Crow Ltd
The Crow's Nest, 10a Lant Street
London SE1 1QR
www.nosycrow.com

ISBN 978 0 85763 886 1

The words 'The National Trust' and the oak leaf logo are registered trademarks
used under licence from National Trust (Enterprises) Limited (Registered Company Number 01083105)

Nosy Crow and associated logos are trademarks and/or registered
trademarks of Nosy Crow Ltd (Registered Company Number 7130282)

Text © Nosy Crow 2017
Illustrations © Sebastien Braun 2017

The right of Nosy Crow to be identified as the author and Sebastien Braun
to be identified as the illustrator of this work has been asserted.

All rights reserved

This book is sold subject to the condition that it shall not, by way of trade or otherwise,
be lent, hired out or otherwise circulated in any form of binding or cover other than that in which it is published.
No part of this publication may be reproduced, stored in a retrieval system, or transmitted in any form or by any means
(electronic, mechanical, photocopying, recording or otherwise) without the prior written permission of Nosy Crow Ltd.

A CIP catalogue record for this book is available from the British Library.

Printed in Turkey

Papers used by Nosy Crow are made from wood grown in sustainable forests.

1 3 5 7 9 8 6 4 2

LOOK AND SAY
WHAT YOU SEE ON THE FARM

Sebastien Braun

It is always busy on the farm!
There is so much to see
and do, all year long.

Can you see . . . ?

cow

horse

magpie

pig

Have you ever been to a farm?

What did you see there?

Little lambs are born in the spring.
Many sheep have two lambs, called twins.

Can you see . . . ?

nest

lamb

donkey

daffodil

Look at the playful lambs jumping about!
What else can you see in the fields?

bluebell

blackbird

primrose

sheep

cherry tree

Look at all the little chicks! How many can you count?

The mother hens peck in the dirt to find grain, worms and bugs to feed their babies.

Can you see . . . ?

chick

cockerel

ant

henhouse

Some hens are sitting on their nests, keeping their eggs warm until they hatch.

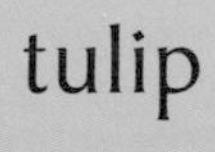

tulip

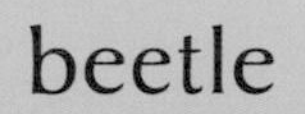

beetle

hen

egg

foxglove

Cows make milk for their babies, called calves. These cows are sharing their milk with the farmer.

Can you see . . . ?

stool

bucket

harvest mouse

cow

The milk is taken to the dairy
to be poured into bottles, or made
into *yogurt*, cheese and ice cream – *yum!*

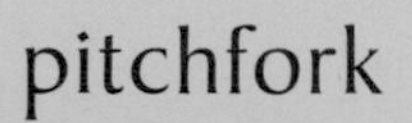
pitchfork

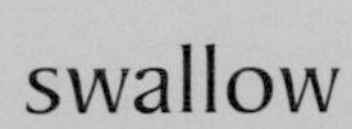
swallow

wellington boots

calf

milk churn

It's a busy morning down at the pond!
This mother duck is teaching her
ducklings to swim. Splish, splash!

Can you see . . . ?

lilypad

trout

duck

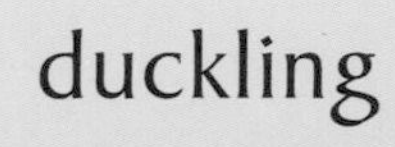

duckling

These baby geese are called goslings. Their grey feathers will soon turn white.

goose gosling tadpole frog minnow

A mother horse is called a mare.

This mare has a new baby, called a foal. The foal can already stand up, even though it has just been born!

Can you see . . . ?

sparrow

helmet

cat

kitten

The mother cat has also had kittens.
What does the cat say?

Nature is an important part of a farm. Hedgerows, and the wild animals, flowers and insects that live there, help to make a farm a happier, healthier place.

Can you see . . . ?

bee

butterfly

fox

beehive

These bees will help crops grow in the fields by carrying pollen from plant to plant.

field maple

vole

blue tit

honeysuckle

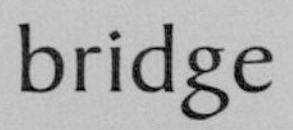

bridge

The vegetable patch is full of delicious things to eat! The plants need lots of sunshine and plenty of water to grow.

Can you see . . . ?

ladybird

caterpillar

tomatoes

carrots

The rabbits would love to nibble on those crunchy carrots!

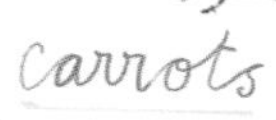

rabbit

snail

marigold

lettuce

watering can

In the autumn, the combine harvester cuts wheat in the fields.

Can you see . . . ?

combine harvester

spider

hoe

barrel

A farmer keeps lots of
useful tools in his shed.
How many can you see?

Who is hiding in the shed?

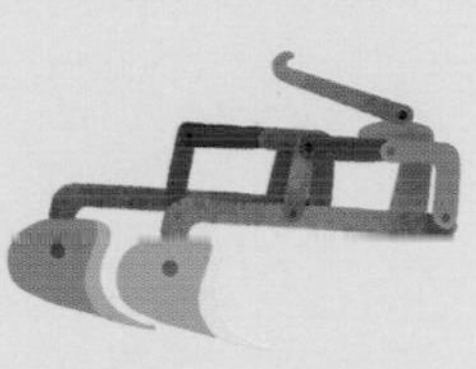

puppy dog rake plough spade

These pigs love rolling in the mud!
Do you like jumping in muddy puddles?

Can you see . . . ?

acorn

piglet

trough

muddy puddle

Pigs like to eat acorns and maize.

crow

pumpkin

corn cob

oak leaf

pig

In the spring, these apple trees are covered with blossom. Over the summer, the flowers will turn into fruit.

In the autumn, the apples are ready to pick. Lots of animals like to live in the orchard!

Can you see . . . ?

apples

finch

ladder

ox-eye daisy

wren
pears
dormouse
cowslip
crate

It is a cold night, but inside the barn it is warm and cosy. All the animals are sleeping now. Shhh!

Can you see . . . ?

lamb

stars

piglet

foal

kid
puppy
chick
calf
owl